CW00505884

Text: *Dennis Kelsall*
Series editor: *Tony Bowerman*
Photographs: *Dennis Kelsall, Chiz Dakin/
www.peakimages.co.uk, John Roger Palmour,
Phil Boland, Steve Fedun, Tony Bowerman,
Shutterstock, Dreamstime*

Design: *Carl Rogers*

Northern Eye Books
ISBN 978-1-908632-05-0

*A CIP catalogue record for this book is available
from the British Library.*

www.northerneyebooks.co.uk

First published in 2013 by

Northern Eye Books Limited

Northern Eye Books, Tattenhall, Cheshire CH3 9PX

Email: tony@northerneyebooks.com

For sales enquiries, please call 01928 723 744

Cover: *Cave Dale at Castleton (Walk 1).*
Photo: John Potter of Doncaster

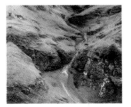

Contents

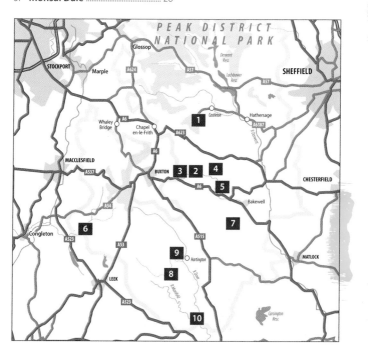

England's first National Park

CREATED IN 1951, THE PEAK DISTRICT NATIONAL PARK extends over six counties and is the second most visited of Britain's National Parks. Its highest point lies upon the seemingly remote Kinder plateau, where a mass trespass in 1932 marked the turning point in a long and sometimes bitter campaign that led to the creation of Britain's National Parks and the open access we enjoy today.

The high, peaty moorlands of the northern Dark Peak are founded on gritstone, their stark grandeur accentuated by impressive weatherworn tors and edges. The moors extend out of the Pennines in two horns that enclose the limestone plateau of the White Peak, an upland pasture cleft by narrow gorges and dales. The transition between the two is startlingly abrupt and each has a distinctive character and beauty all its own; the wild openness of the north contrasting with a more intimate landscape dotted with small villages and criss-crossed by old lanes.

Monsal Dale and Upperdale from Monsal Head

Dales and Valleys

The White Peak is known for dramatic limestone gorges: convoluted pathways carved into its heart, where rearing pinnacles, dark caves and thundering rivers struck awe into seventeenth-century travellers. Still captivating today, they harbour rich woodland, wildflower meadows and disappearing and resurgent streams, one of the area's strangest curiosities.

Delightful Dovedale, once the haunt of the renowned anglers Izaak Walton and Charles Cotton, contrasts with Cave Dale, a gaunt, dry passage below Castleton's Norman stronghold. But the Dark Peak has attractive valleys too, and different again is the Dane Valley, which cuts onto the Cheshire Plain from the gritstone moors.

> "He that has seen Dovedale has no need to visit the Highlands."

Boswell's *Life of Johnson*, 1774

TOP 10 **Walks:** Dales and Valleys

ALTHOUGH KNOWN AS THE PEAKS, it is perhaps in the deep dales and valleys cleaving the high limestone plateau that some of the Peak District's prettiest scenery is to be found. There is variety too: some of the dales are dry while others contain crystal-clear rivers and streams, and thick woods that give way to steep-sided flower meadows. These walks are among my personal favourites and reflect an intimate quality within the National Park.

Cave Dale & Winnat's Pass — page 8

Monk's Dale — page 12

Chee Dale — page 16

Miller's Dale — page 22

Winnats Pass and Mam Tor

Cave Dale & Winnats Pass

An uncomplicated circuit combining the two dramatic gorges that cleave the limestone hills overlooking Castleton

What to expect:
Good paths and tracks, short road section. Steady ascent along Cave Dale

Distance/time: 7km/4½ miles. Allow 2¼ hours

Start: Castleton Visitor Centre beside the town's main pay and display car park

Grid ref: SK 149 829

Ordnance Survey Map: Explorer OL1 *The Peak District: Dark Peak area: Kinder Scout, Bleaklow, Black Hill & Ladybower Reservoir*

After the walk: Choice of pubs and cafés around the town

Walk outline

The walk leaves the town on a climbing path through Cave Dale, passing beneath the ruins of the town's ancient castle. Picking up old walled tracks, the way continues between upland fields to the head of Winnats Pass. Joining the lane, it heads down through the gorge to the Speedwell Cavern. The final leg gives fine views across to Mam Tor as it contours the hillside to the Peak Cavern, just above the town.

Castleton and its caves

Castleton sits below the edge of the Peakland limestone plateau looking across the Hope Valley to an impressive backdrop of Mam Tor and Lose Hill. The hills behind the town are honeycombed with caves and tunnels, some natural, but others dug over the centuries by miners in search of metal ore and minerals. Castleton is unique in Britain for having four show caves on its doorstep. The Peak Cavern, also known as the Devil's Arse, burrows beneath Peveril Castle and at one time housed a pub within its massive entrance. Speedwell, also passed on the walk, was worked as a lead mine, but has since flooded and can now be visited only by boat.

Mam Tor subsidence

Raven

The Walk

1. From the **Visitor Centre**, walk into town. At a bend, turn right past **St Edmund's Church**. Approaching the top, keep left past a green, once the site of the town's market, and bear left again into **Bargate**.

2. After 100 metres, branch right along a short, narrow street between cottages. Pass beneath rocky buttresses to a gate, from which a winding path begins a steady climb into **Cave Dale**. High above is the gaunt ruin of **Peveril Castle**, best seen in retrospect farther on. Progressing through a gate gap into the upper valley, the gradient eases as the gorge shallows towards its head.

3. At the top, beyond a couple of gates, the path diverges from the right-hand wall across the crest of the field. The impressive hill to the north is **Mam Tor,** the embanked defences of a prehistoric settlement clearly visible around its summit. Leave the far corner of the field through a couple of gates onto a walled track.

4. Turn right through a gate. Shortly reaching a fork in front of a second gate, take the right branch. Walk for 1.5km/1 mile, passing **Rowter Farm** and ultimately meeting a lane.

5. Go right to a junction and right again, the way signed to 'Castleton'. Initially there is no verge, but shortly, beyond a cattlegrid, the bounding walls end to open a grass swathe into the deepening gorge of **Winnats Pass**.

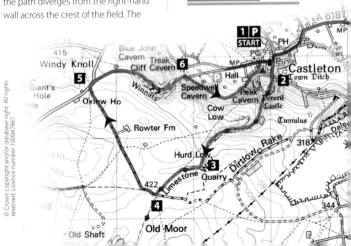

Mountain high?: *The giddy view down into Winnats Pass*

6. Beyond the entrance to the **Speedwell Cavern**, leave the lane through a gate on the right onto the National Trust's Long Cliff. A clear path leads along the edge of rough pasture. Ahead, the squat tower of **Peveril Castle** peeks through skyline trees while grassed heaps indicate lead mining across the hillside. Exit the fields through a gate below a wood and walk past cottages towards the town. A street to the right leads to the **Peak Cavern** at the base of a towering cliff, but the way back lies ahead. After crossing a bridge, go left beside the stream to meet the main road opposite the Visitor Centre, to complete the walk. ♦

Peveril Castle

Making the most of the natural defences afforded by the deep gorge of Cave Dale, this small castle was founded around 1085 by William Peveril, one of William's loyal supporters during the Norman invasion of England. The Peverils held extensive tracts of land in the Midlands, including Nottingham Castle, and the stronghold here was used as an administrative centre and hunting lodge for the royal Forest of High Peak.

Wildflower-rich limestone grassland in Monk's Dale

Monk's Dale

Ancient native woodland and flower-rich grasslands thrive in this National Nature Reserve

What to expect:
Clear tracks and paths; Monk's Dale path is rough and slippery after rain

Distance/time: 6.5km/4 miles. Allow 2 hours

Start: Miller's Dale pay and display car park at former station yard, off the B6049, east of village

Grid ref: SK 138 732

Ordnance Survey Map: Explorer OL24 *Peak District: White Peak area: Buxton, Bakewell, Matlock & Dovedale*

After the walk: The Angler's Rest pub beside the River Wye in Miller's Dale

Walk outline

The walk begins along a former railway, passing disused quarries and lime kilns before dropping across the river beside an ancient mill. Climbing to the high ground, old tracks lead to the head of the dale and give fine views across the countryside. A rough, woodland path winds back through the dale where a profusion of wildflowers and the resurgence of underground streams are amongst things to look out for.

Monk's Dale

Monk's Dale lies within the Derbyshire Dales National Nature Reserve and was formed by surging meltwater as the glaciers receded. Sheltered by limestone cliffs are contrasting habitats—dense, moss-cloaked ash woods and limestone grassland, rich in wildflowers, birds and insects.

Flowers such as wood anemone and yellow archangel appear in early spring, while the steep meadows come into their own in early summer, when cowslips, early-purple- and common spotted orchids bloom. The wildflowers attract butterflies too; look for the northern brown argus, whose caterpillars eat the leaves of the common rock rose.

Drystone waller

Nettle-leaved bellflower

The Walk

1. Leave the car park onto the platform of the old station to join the **Monsal Trail** and follow it left over a **viaduct**. After 400 metres/¼ mile, past the **Miller's Dale Quarry** and lime kilns, watch for a signpost to 'Miller's Dale' marking a path off to the left. Drop to a bridge across the **River Wye** and walk out to a lane, there going left past the site of the old mill to the B6049.

2. Turn right along the road, but then branch left up a steep, narrow lane. After 150 metres, double back left on a gated track that climbs to **Monksdale Farm**. In the yard, swing left to a gate by the farmhouse. Signed the 'Limestone Way', the onward track rises more gently between walled upper pastures, in time reaching a junction.

3. Go left and walk for almost another 800 metres/½ mile to emerge at a junction of lanes by **Monksdale House**. Turn left, descending into the dale.

4. At the bottom of the hill, leave through a gap stile on the left and cross a small meadow towards the narrowing confines of **Monk's Dale**. A rocky and uneven path twists between the trees, following the course of a normally dry streambed into the nature reserve. Take care, for the stones can be slippery. Beyond a wall gap, the path forks, the main branch rising over a bluff overlooking the resurgence of the spring.

Eventually leaving the woods, the valley opens to rising meadows and scree. The path again splits, the main branch

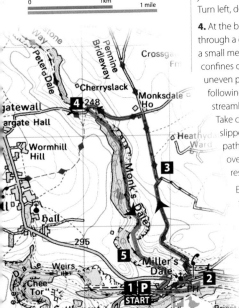

Deep and damp: *Moss, roots and boulders shape the rocky path through Monk's Dale*

taking a higher line to give a fine view back up the dale. Path and stream later come together once more, leading you to a **footbridge**.

5. Continue on the opposite bank until path and stream part company. The way angles up the hillside, emerging into the corner of a meadow by a wall. Ignoring a gate, turn right, rising towards farm buildings. Leave the nature reserve through a gate and follow a short contained path past **Glebe Farm** to come out onto a lane. Walk left down the hill back to the car park to complete the walk. ♦

Scented beauty

Amongst the many woodland wildflowers that flourish in Monk's Dale is the rare lily of the valley, whose white, bell-shaped flowers appear in May and symbolise purity. Their lovely, subtle scent is used as a fragrance and although poisonous, the plant was once used to treat medical complaints including gout and memory loss, while its juices dabbed on the neck supposedly imparted common sense.

Unusual riverside stepping stones wind through Chee Dale

Chee Dale

One of the Peak's most dramatic gorges, so narrow that the path resorts to stepping stones along the river

What to expect:
Uneven path through the gorge; stepping-stones can be flooded after heavy rain

Distance/time: 7km/4½ miles. Allow 2½ hours

Start: Miller's Dale pay and display car park at former station yard, off B6049, east of village.

Grid ref: SK 138 732

Ordnance Survey Map: Explorer OL24 *Peak District: White Peak area: Buxton, Bakewell, Matlock & Dovedale*

After the walk: Lazy Days Tuck Shop at Blackwell Mill and riverside Angler's Rest pub in Miller's Dale

Walk outline

After beginning along a disused railway, the route drops to an attractive riverside path through Chee Dale. In places, the path clambers over rocks and twice resorts to stepping stones, but reveals some of the most impressive aspects of the gorge. At Blackwell, the way climbs from the river onto the Monsal Trail and follows the old railway through tunnels and over viaducts all the way back to Miller's Dale.

Chee Dale

Although only 24 kilometres/15 miles long, the Wye is regarded as one of Derbyshire's prettiest rivers and flows through a succession of winding dales, each blessed with a different character. The most dramatic of these is Chee Dale, a narrow gorge defined by overhanging limestone cliffs that soar 30 metres above the river.

The valley provided a route for the railway from Derby to Buxton, but the twisted confines of Chee Dale posed a challenge and the engineers had to burrow beneath the gaunt outcrop of Chee Tor. With the closure of the railway, the tunnel was sealed, but has recently been re-opened to provide a foot and cycleway through the valley.

Rusher Cutting Tunnel

Limestone meadow

The Walk

1. From the car park, join the railway track-bed and follow it to the right, past the station platform. The route is signposted as the 'Monsal Trail to Chee Dale and Buxton'. The Trail passes disused quarries and a lime kiln.

Both mining and quarrying have been carried out around the Peak since antiquity, but workings were generally small-scale, held back by, amongst other things, an economic means of transporting heavy and bulky products to the industrial centres.

Beyond the **East Buxton Lime Kilns**, continue to a high **railway viaduct**, which takes the track-bed across the

River Wye towards the eastern portal of the **Chee Tor Tunnel**.

In 1796, the construction of the Peak Forest Canal and a connecting tramway enabled the development of the Dove Holes quarries, north east of Buxton, but it was the arrival of the railway that enabled exploitation here on an industrial scale. The track through Chee Dale to Buxton from Derby was completed in 1863, with an extension north through Great Rocks Dale and the Dove Holes Tunnel to Manchester being opened two years later.

2. Immediately before the viaduct, leave the Monsal Trail, descending steeply down steps to the riverbank. Walk upstream beside the **Wye**, shortly

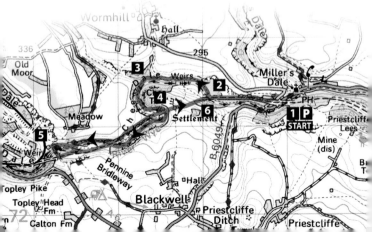

Exciting stuff: *Stepping stones traverse the riverside below Chee Dale's limestone cliffs*

reaching a footbridge. However, do not cross, but instead continue ahead into the **Chee Dale Nature Reserve**.

3. Before long, the path is forced from the river to avoid the tufa encrusted resurgence of **Wormhill Springs** at the foot of Flag Dale. *These springs are one of the largest upwellings from the Peak District limestone, discharging more than 10 million gallons a day.*

After crossing a footbridge over a side stream, the path returns to the main valley and heads into the confines of **Chee Dale**. Easy clambering takes the way beneath dripping, overhung cliffs of limestone, but the gorge eventually becomes so constricted that the path is forced onto stepping stones along the riverbed. Providing these are not covered, it is safe to carry on, but be careful of your footing.

4. Regaining solid ground, cross a footbridge below a high viaduct over which the railway enters the western end of the **Chee Tor Tunnel**. The path

Dawn's early light: *The first rays of the sun illuminate the rim of Chee Dale at dawn*

continues upstream above the river, passing a junction that leads back up to the **Monsal Trail** before dropping to another footbridge. Keep going beside the Wye, where you might spot jumping trout in the deeper pools. After a second stretch of stepping stones, the path again swaps banks, eventually returning to the northern side of the valley. Joining the **Pennine Bridleway**, it leads to cottages at **Blackwell Mill**. Cross the bridge to a turning area, which is overlooked by the **Lazy Days Tuck Shop and Cycle Hire**.

5. Following a sign to the 'Monsal Trail', walk up beside the cabin. Join the course of the old railway line through a gate and go left towards 'Bakewell'. Although closely paralleling your outward route, the elevated track gives a completely different perspective of the gorge, with the river now far below in the trees.

After crossing the **viaduct**, the track passes through two short tunnels whose signs are painted in the old Midland Railway livery colours. A second viaduct takes the route through the well-lit **Chee Tor Tunnel**, which runs in a gentle curve for 400 metres beneath the hill.

6. Emerging into daylight, cross a final **viaduct** and return along your outward route past the **East Buxton Lime Kilns.**

The kilns were built in 1880 and continued in operation until 1944. The two adjacent kilns were worked continually; one being emptied and then filled while the other burned.

Continue to **Miller's Dale Station**, to complete the walk. ◆

Lime kilns

Lime had long been used as a fertiliser on fields and in the production of mortar, but the arrival of the Industrial Age demanded vast quantities for the production of steel. The limestone cliffs on both sides of the valley overlooking Miller's Dale were extensively quarried and giant kilns built beside the track so that the burnt lime could be shovelled directly into waiting railway wagons.

Swans and still waters in tranquil Miller's Dale

Miller's Dale

A superb walk incorporating five pretty dales, where relics of industry reveal a very different past

What to expect:
Clear paths; Water-Cum-Jolly Dale may be flooded after rain; short sections on quiet lanes

Distance/time: 9km/5¾miles. Allow 3 hours

Start: Tideswell Dale pay and display car park

Grid ref: SK 154 742

Ordnance Survey Map: Explorer OL24 *Peak District: White Peak area: Buxton, Bakewell, Matlock & Dovedale*

After the walk: Pubs and café in Tideswell

Walk outline

After exploring an abandoned quarry, the route meanders through Tideswell Dale to Miller's Dale. A riverside stroll through Water-cum-Jolly Dale leads from Litton Mill to Cressbrook Mil, before climbing into Cressbrook Dale. Beyond the tiny settlement of Ravensdale, a woodland path continues into the dale's higher reaches, turning up Tansley Dale towards Litton. The final return is via field paths and a lane.

Miller's Dale

The quiet seclusion found in many of the Peak's dales belies their past and Miller's Dale is no exception. Two hundred years ago, the valley was teeming with industry, with water-driven mills producing flour, timber, silk and cotton. There was even a factory distilling oils from lavender, peppermint and other herbs.

Small grist mills had been a feature throughout the Middle Ages, but the impetus for industrialisation was the improvement of roads during the late eighteenth century. Cressbrook Mill and Litton Mill were built in the 1780s to produce fine cotton yarn and remained in production into the second half of the twentieth century.

Cressbrook Dale footbridge

Kingfisher

The Walk

1. A path leaves beside the toilets. Through a gate, branch left on a rising track to the quarry. At the top, continue through a second gate across the meadowed quarry floor to the working face. *Curiously, the rock is dolerite, the result of an intrusive magma sill welling through the limestone and spreading across a horizontal fault.*

2. Veer right along a grass track and bear right again to follow a fence, from which there is a view to the valley below. Pass through a hand gate at the far end, losing height steeply to rejoin the main path through the dale.

3. Emerging onto a lane, walk left to **Litton Mill**.

4. Continue ahead through the gates past the mill building, winding over a bridge across the tail race to continue down-river. *Farther along is the ruin of a small water mill, its skeletal wheel still in place below the weir.* The path eventually curves beneath the overhanging cliffs surrounding **Cressbrook's mill pond**. If the path is flooded, an alternative route is signed just before the cliffs, which clambers up the steep bank

Dappled sunlight: *Walking alongside the River Wye in leafy Miller's Dale*

below **Cressbrook Hall**. Coming out onto a lane go right and at the bottom of the hill, turn left to rejoin the walk at (**5**). Over a bridge at the far side of the millpond, follow the millrace towards the mill, swinging left behind it along a contained path out to the lane.

5. Turn left up the lane, taking the right fork towards 'Cressbrook and Litton'. Climb steadily uphill for nearly 800 metres/½ mile to reach a side lane off to Ravensdale.

6. Drop to the cottages huddled below the towering white wall of **Raven Cliff**, keeping ahead along a path into the wooded valley. After crossing a bridge into the **Cressbrook Dale Nature Reserve**, the path shortly forks. That ahead continues through thicket, while the other ascends to the rim of the valley where there is a magnificent vantage point. *Clearly visible are old lead workings that follow the vein of ore crossing the valley.*

The two paths converge back at the base of the valley. Carry on a little farther

Limestone dale: *Looking across drystone-walled fields into the head of Tansley Dale*

to find a **bridge** across the usually dry stream bed in front of a small wall gate.

7. With time to spare, you might first continue into the upper valley to see **Peter's Stone (8)**, an impressive dome of limestone that has slipped from the adjacent hillside. *Known locally as Gibbet Rock, it was once topped with a wooden gibbet and iron cage in which the corpses of executed criminals were hung in chains to deter others.* Otherwise pass through the gate and head up **Tansley Dale**, which also bears the muted scars of

old lead workings. Towards the top, the path climbs out right to a stile. Head diagonally right across pasture, swinging past the corner of a wall to a stile beside a gate at the far end of the field. Emerging onto a track, follow it left to come out onto the bend of a lane at the edge of **Litton**.

9. Walk forward to the next bend, and abandon the lane through a squeeze stile facing you. Walk on at the edge of successive fields and then along a fenced path, which winds out to a second lane. Cross to the gate and stile opposite and follow the field edge straight downhill, exiting at the bottom

beside a house onto another lane. Go left down **Litton Dale**.

10. Reaching a junction with the B6049 at the bottom, turn left. Almost immediately, leave through a gated squeeze stile on the left and continue along a narrow roadside meadow below limestone crags and scree. Pass out through a gate at the bottom and follow a line of beech trees back to the car park to complete the walk. ♦

Miller and Cressbrook Dales' mills

Even by the harsh standards of its day, Litton Mill had a bad reputation, paying rock bottom wages and drafting orphan children from London workhouses to work as virtual slaves. The mill was eventually taken over by a more enlightened master who installed an auxiliary steam engine. By the end of the nineteenth-century, Litton and Cressbrook mills had a single owner. The mills worked into the 1960s, processing cotton, silk, and artificial fibres.

Upperdale from Monsal Head

Monsal Dale

An enjoyable walk combining open hillside and riverside woodland

What to expect:
Steady climb at start of walk

Distance: 5.5km/3½ miles. Allow 2 hours

Start: White Lodge pay and display car park

Grid ref: SK 170 706

Ordnance Survey Map: Explorer OL24 *Peak District: White Peak area: Buxton, Bakewell, Matlock & Dovedale*

After the walk: Ashford Arms or Bull's Head pubs at Ashford in the Water

Walk outline

A steep woodland path takes the route out of the valley to Brushfield Hough, before picking up a good track that wanders across hilltop fields. Later descending to the River Wye at Upperdale, there is an opportunity to walk onto the famous viaduct. Dropping to join a riverside path, the way passes under the towering bridge to continue along the pretty, winding dale back to the start.

Monsal Head

Monsal Head is one of the Peak District's celebrated viewpoints and looks down upon a sweeping horseshoe bend of the River Wye. Below is the Headstone Viaduct, built in 1863 as part of the Midland Railway's push for a line between London and Manchester.

Routing the line through the snaking gorge posed many problems, demanding complex tunnelling and bold bridges. The five arches of the 100-metre long viaduct straddle the valley, carrying the line some twelve metres above the Wye. The riverside path beneath emphasises the engineering challenge, while a short detour takes you up to the viewpoint overlooking the viaduct.

Headstone Viaduct

Wild arum in autumn

The Walk

1. A path drops from the car park's information board to the main A6 road.

Cross carefully, go through a gap stile opposite, and walk down a meadow to cross a stream and stile. At a junction a few metres farther on, take the second left: a stepped path that plods up through the trees towards 'Brushfield Hough'. At the top, emerging into more open ground, carry on to find a wall stile.

2. Join a track to go right towards **Brushfield Hough Farm**. Approaching the entrance, bear off to a second gateway just to the left. Pass through a gate into a yard, winding left and then right to walk away behind a long barn, on a gravel track.

Leaving the farm behind, continue along the edge of the pasture. Passing into a second field, bear away towards a gap in the top righthand corner.

3. Turn right again, along a track signed to 'Upperdale', which wanders easily above the valley giving fine views across the countryside.

Just over a kilometre/¾ mile later, the ground falls away past old quarry workings, and the track descends to a junction.

4. Keep ahead on a bridleway that

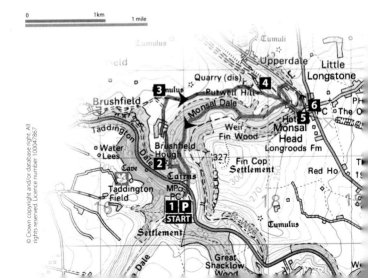

Valley view: *The lovely wooded limestone valley of Upperdale*

runs down through scrub to meet the **Monsal Trail** beside the **viaduct**.

But first turn right, and walk across the viaduct to the portal of the **Monsal Tunnel** for wonderful views.

The 19th-century poet Eliza Cook wrote of Monsal:

> And Monsal, thou mine of Arcadian treasure
> Need we seek for Greek Islands and spice-laden gales
> Whilst a temple like thine of enchantment and pleasure
> May be found in our own native Derbyshire Dales?

The influential Victorian writer and art critic John Ruskin was equally enchanted by the place and a vociferous opponent of the railway's routing through the valley in 1863. He labelled the viaduct an ugly intrusion and wrote '…and now, every fool in Buxton can be in Bakewell in half an hour, and every fool in Bakewell at Buxton; which you think a lucrative process of exchange—you Fools everywhere.'

Monsal Head panorama: *The famous Headstone Viaduct below Monsal Head*

I wonder how he would have viewed the HS2 links north from London?

But the line remained in operation for over a century and the view from the carriages as the train emerged from Monsal Tunnel was surely a highlight of the trip.

5. Once you've had a good look, return across the viaduct and immediately drop right on a descending path down to the **River Wye**, below.

To reach **Monsal Head (6)**, where there is a pub and viewpoint, cross the bridge and continue to a junction by a cottage. Turn right and follow a steeply rising path up the side of the valley.

Otherwise, stay on this bank and follow the riverside path beneath the viaduct and on down **Monsal Dale**.

The spectacular 8½ mile/13 kilometre long Monsal Trail is immensely popular with walkers, cyclists and horseriders. It follows a section of the old Manchester, Buxton, Matlock and Midland Junction Railway closed by Barbara Castle in 1968. Although the Trail was officially opened by the Peak District National Park Authority in 1981 the main tunnels have been passable

only since 2011. It is now possible to walk or cycle all the way from Bakewell to Blackwell Mill (see the Chee Dale walk).

The way continues pleasantly through waterside meadows and then the fringes of woodland for around another 2.5 kilometres/1½ miles. Ultimately reaching a junction at the edge of the wood, retrace your outward steps back to the car park to complete the walk. ♦

Monsal Dale

Monsal Dale's steep slopes support a mix of semi-natural woodland and ungrazed scrub and grassland, which supports a rich variety of plant-life. Ash, wych elm and clumps of hawthorn are common while arum, wood anemone, violets and even wild strawberry are amongst the smaller plants to be found. In areas where lead mining has taken place, you may come across the nationally scarce leadwort.

Sunlight dapples the fast-flowing River Dane near Barleighford

Dane Valley

A scenic walk beside the River Dane as it breaks from the western gritstone edge of the Peak

What to expect:
Generally good tracks and field paths, with an undemanding ascent from the valley

Distance/time: 6.5km/4 miles. Allow 2 hours

Start: Dane Bridge. Broad roadside parking area at bridge foot

Grid ref: SJ 965 651

Ordnance Survey Map: Explorer OL24 *Peak District: White Peak area: Buxton, Bakewell, Matlock & Dovedale*

After the walk: The Ship Inn, Danebridge. Closed on Mondays

Walk outline

After wandering through riverside meadows to the site of an old mill, the route crosses the Dane to follow a feeder canal above the river. Later climbing from the valley, the way back tackles the hillside overlooking Shell Brook to Wincle Grange, returning through the village past the Ship Inn.

River Dane

The River Dane is one of four that has its source on Axe Edge Moor. It winds for 56 kilometres/35 miles through the Cheshire countryside before merging with the River Weaver and ultimately the Mersey to escape to the sea.

Ship Inn at Danebridge

Like the River Goyt, the Dane flows through the gritstone of the Dark Peak. At Dane Bridge, it leaves the peat and heather moorland of its upper reaches for a more pastoral countryside of wooded valleys and grazing pastures.

The origins of the river's name are obscure and may refer to the 9th-century Scandinavian settlement of the area or perhaps to *Danu*, a Celtic water deity and mother goddess.

Goosander and young

Monastic farm: *Wincle Grange farm was built by Combermere Abbey, around 1400*

The Walk

1. Leave the lane by the bridge near the telephone box on a track to **Danebridge Fisheries**. It leads past the Wincle Beer Company's brewhouse and then a fishing lake and trout farm.

Approaching a cottage, take the parallel footpath to bypass the yard, walking through a gate into open pasture. A trod guides the way across, as the river meanders off to the left, continuing through a second meadow. Close with the river at the far side to pass a **weir** above the site of Whitelee Mill, below **Gig Hall**. Carry on downstream past a second weir and cross a **footbridge**.

Several mills were once turned by the Dane's rushing waters. The one below Gig Hall was originally built to serve the monastic granges in the area. Once a gig mill used for fulling cloth, it was rebuilt as a paper mill in the 18th century.

Keep an eye out for unusual, originally northern ducks called goosanders, which have bred on the Dane since around 2003.

2. Turn right on a footpath signposted to 'Barleighford Bridge', which runs alongside a disued feeder canal.

The conduit was constructed at the beginning of the 19th century to feed water to Rudyard Lake, built as a reservoir for the Caldon Canal, a branch of the Trent and Mersey Canal.

Through a gate, continue past a cottage, later passing a stone bridge. Keep going, eventually crossing a stile beside a second bridge onto a track. Leaving the **Dane Valley Way**, follow the track downhill to a bridge spanning the **River Dane** at **Barleighford**.

3. Cross the river and remain with the rising track to a bend. Leave ahead over a stile beside a gate, waymarked for the Gritstone Trail, and, bearing slightly right, carry on up the

loosely wooded meadow of the hill. The ground falls away below into the deep fold of the **Shell Brook valley**.

The prominent hill out to the left is The Cloud, straddling the border between Staffordshire and Cheshire.

The way later crosses springs seeping from the rock on a succession of boardwalks before passing through a kissing-gate and then over a stile. As a view opens to The Roaches, ignore a stile off on the right and walk on past an abandoned barn to a fork.

0   1km
          1 mile

Slopes and valleys: *The Gritstone Trail crosses pastures above the Shell Brook valley*

4. Keep ahead over a stile and head up through trees along an old **sunken way**. As the way opens out, stay with the line of trees to a stile beside a gate and continue up at edge of the next field.

Broaching the rise, **Wincle Grange** comes into view ahead, the path curving left to dip across a stream. *Wincle Grange was built around 1400 by the monks of Combermere Abbey in Cheshire, whose founder, Hugh de Malbanc, owned Wincle manor. Although much altered in 1670, the grange retains many medieval*

architectural features such as window tracery and mouldings.

Carry on, passing the farm, just beyond which a stile leads onto a lane beside its entrance.

5. Follow the lane to the right past a pond. *Staffordshire's iconic Roaches and Hen Cloud are visible ahead, while the distinctive, isolated conical summit out to the left is Cheshire's very own Matterhorn: Shutlingsloe.*

Leave the lane just after the bend through a gated stile on the right. Bear left downfield, continuing over a stile to drop more steeply through

a wood. Carry on at the edge of the pasture beyond to find a stile in the accompanying wall. Cross over a drive to a stile opposite and head out across the corner of a meadow to a final stile. Back on the lane, walk right past the **Ship Inn** down to **Dane Bridge** to complete the walk. ♦

The Ship Inn

The sign above the door shows the schooner Nimrod *anchored off Cape Royds during Shackleton's first expedition to Antarctica in 1908. Among the party was Sir Philip Brocklehurst of Swythamley Hall, who had paid to join the expedition as Assistant Geologist. However, as the pub long predates the expedition and has connections with Bonnie Prince Charlie, it's more likely the name is simply a corruption of 'shippen' or barn.*

Crystal clear waters in Lathkill Dale

Lathkill Dale

Wander through one of the Peak's finest limestone dales, famed for its woodland, wildflowers and crystal waters

What to expect:
*Easy field and riverside paths.. **Note**: Dogs must be kept on short leads in Lathkill Dale*

Distance/time: 9.5km/6 miles. Allow 3 hours

Start: Over Haddon, pay and display car park

Grid ref: SK 203 664

Ordnance Survey Map: Explorer OL24 *Peak District: White Peak area: Buxton, Bakewell, Matlock & Dovedale*

After the walk: Lathkill Hotel, Over Haddon

Walk outline

A lane from the village winds down to the river, the continuing path climbing the other side of the valley. Field paths interspersed with another spot of lane walking take the route over the hill to Calling Low, then downhill into Cales Dale. Following the valley into Lathkill Dale, the route wanders easily beside the river to Lathkill Lodge. A short pull back up the hill returns you to the car park.

Lathkill Dale

Lathkill Dale is one of the Peak's little gems, rugged and wild in its upper reaches, wooded and secretive in the middle and quite pastoral farther downstream. The walk showcases the central section, but the extremities beg for exploration too, and those with time to spare will be well rewarded.

The dale's remote beauty disguises an industrial past. Derbyshire 'marble' was quarried at its upper end, while mines tapped veins of lead-rich ore. But there was a gentler side too; until the Second World War there was a working sheep wash at the foot of Cales Dale. The river also supports a unique strain of distinctly red, brown trout.

Conksbury Bridge

Dipper

The Walk

1. Out of the car park, turn right and follow the lane to the river. Over a **clapper bridge** beside the ford, a track winds left and then right up the wooded valley side. Through a gate at the top, strike half-left to the farm at **Meadow Place Grange**.

2. Pass between barns into a central yard, crossing to a high stile beside a barn opposite. Walk up to the field above, keeping briefly beside the righthand wall before striking out at a signpost towards 'Middleton'. Over a stile part-way along the far wall, maintain the line to the top corner of the next field, continuing across a final field to **Back Lane**.

3. Cross to the stile opposite and follow a trod towards a strip of woodland concealing the **Long Rake workings** that exploited a vein of calcite.

Still mined farther to the north, calcite's uses include path chippings and pebbledash, and giving white road lines their reflectivity.

Through the trees, carry on across a second field to emerge on **Moor Lane**. Turn right and walk 400 metres/¼ mile to a junction with the main lane.

4. From a stile on the opposite side of the road, a path strikes diagonally away.

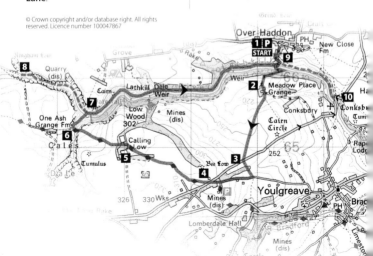

Pure water: *Clear water tumbles over low falls in lovely Lathkill Dale*

Across the field to the right is Bee Low, a late Neolithic/early Bronze Age burial mound, or tumulus, excavated in 1966-8.

Negotiate a stile just left of the far corner and cut right to a second stile. Continue the diagonal course, heading for the distant trees of **Low Moor Wood**. Follow a path between the trees and stride out across the field beyond towards **Calling Low Farm**.

5. Leave the field just before the corner through a kissing-gate on the right. Walk away to find a second gate on the left into the tail of **Bee Low Wood**. Pass through to a small paddock and then into more trees, emerging into another field at the far side.

Head away beside the righthand wall to a kissing-gate and bear left downfield. Keep the same descending line across two more fields to reach a kissing-gate above the wooded gorge of **Cales Dale**.

A stepped path drops steeply through scrub to the bottom of the gorge.

It's gorge-ous: *Looking down into Lathkill Dale from the popular Limestone Way*

6. At a fingerpost over a stile, turn right and head down the valley to a bridge at the bottom spanning the **River Lathkill**.

The upper dale to the left is in stark contrast to the ancient broadleaved woodland of the central section. Wildflower-rich limestone grassland cloaks the valley sides, while in nearby Ricklow Quarry, the rock is rich in fossils.

7. Over the bridge, if not first detouring up to have a look at **Ricklow Quarry (8)**, the onward route lies to the right, shortly passing a pretty tufa waterfall.

Downstream is a man-made weir where Carter's Mill once stood. *Look for a pair of abandoned millstones beside the path. Beyond that are the vestiges of mine workings; a grille-covered shaft and the mounds of spoil heaps.*

Soon after, a bridge leads to **Bateman's House**. *It originally stood over an underground pump house built to drain the workings.*

The onward route, however, remains on the river's northern bank. *The way passes high stone trestles that carried a wooden aqueduct to feed a waterwheel at the Mandale Mine, whose ruined buildings are then seen on the left.*

Walk 7 – **Lathkill Dale** ♦ 45

Leaving the trees behind, the path finally ends at a lane.

9. You can extend the riverside walk to **Conksbury Bridge (10)**, where the clear flow tumbles over a shallow staircase of weirs to create trout pools.

Otherwise, turn left up the hill back to **Over Haddon** to complete the walk. ♦

Mines, metal and money

The rich seams of lead ore running through the Lathkill valley have been mined since antiquity, but flooding was always a problem and ultimately contributed to the industry's demise. In 1854, gold was discovered in the valley too, sparking something of a mini gold-rush. Ironically, the quantity found was so small that money was lost rather than fortunes made.

The dramatic Manifold Valley

Manifold Valley

A pleasant valley walk, returning over the superb viewpoint of Ecton Hill

What to expect:

Level walking along tracks in the Manifold Valley, a steep climb and field paths on the hill

Distance/time: 9.5km/6 miles. Allow 3 hours

Start: Hulme End pay and display car park

Grid ref: SK 102 593

Ordnance Survey Map: Explorer OL24 *Peak District: White Peak area: Buxton, Bakewell, Matlock & Dovedale*

After the walk: Tea rooms at Hulme End and Wetton Mill

Walk outline

Setting out along the Manifold Trail, the way soon joins the River Hamps to Dale Bridge. It then climbs onto Ecton Hill for some easy field walking past disused mines to Broad Ecton Farm, from which there is an enjoyable descent along a secluded valley past the prominent outcrop of the Sugarloaf. After diverting to the river at Wetton Mill, the return follows an old lane before finally rejoining the Manifold Trail.

The Manifold Trail

The Leek and Manifold Light Railway opened in 1904 to transport milk from the valley's farms and a creamery at Ecton and, although built for economy to a narrow gauge, main line tankers were carried to and from Ecton on specially built transporter wagons.

Castle Folly

The hope that it might also revitalise Ecton Hill's copper mines came to naught, but weekends and bank holidays saw it busy with passengers escaping the pottery towns. The closure of the creamery in 1932 left the line unprofitable and it finally closed in 1934. However, just three years later Staffordshire County Council opened it as the Manifold Trail, the country's first such leisure trail.

Small copper butterfly

The Walk

1. Follow the **Manifold Trail** from the car park, sweeping across the fields and then joining the river to meet a lane at **Dale Bridge**.

2. Leaving the Trail, go left to a junction. Turn right but then immediately branch left up a rough lane signed to 'Top of Ecton and Wetton'.

At the **Castle Folly**, with its distinctive copper-clad spire (built in 1933 by Arthur Radcliffe, the MP for Leek), leave the track beneath the archway onto the adjacent path. Over a stile, head straight up the hillside, ascending steeply beside the boundary to a stone building, the former **engine house** for the Ecton Hill mines.

Mining on Ecton Hill goes back to the Middle Ages, but it was only during the 18th century under the Devonshires of Chatsworth that operations assumed an industrial scale. Although lead and zinc were found too, the main prize was copper. The ores here were some of the richest in Europe, sometimes yielding up to 60% metal!

Following vertical pipes of ore, the workings were some of the deepest for their time, and a veritable maze of shafts, levels and adits honeycomb the hill. It was one of the first mines to use gunpowder for underground blasting, steam engines were employed both for winding ore to the surface and to pump water from the

Engine house: *A steam engine inside this hut once raised water and ore from the mine*

lower workings and in some places, ore was moved in boats along underground canals .

Production peaked at over 4,000 tons a year, making a small fortune for the Devonshires and reputedly furnishing the money for the construction of the famous Crescent at Bath.

Carry on past the building to the wall corner. Ignoring the gates, swing right and resume climbing alongside the wall past the capped mine shafts. Through a gate at the top, bear right on a rising path. Cross a broken wall and continue to the summit.

3. Beyond the Ordnance Survey 'trig' point, bear left off the ridge across open pasture towards the ruin of a barn. Pass it on your right and walk on by the right wall towards more mine workings.

There, cross a stile and immediately turn right through a wicket gate signed to 'Old Ecton'. Head down the field to **Broad Ecton Farm**, keeping ahead over a stile to meet the corner of a track.

Manifold Destiny: *A broad panorama seen from the slopes above the Manifold Valley*

4. Follow the track left from the farm to a bend. Leave through a gate on the right and walk away by the wall into the descending fold of a valley.

Lower down, cross a squeeze stile onto the National Trust's **Dale Farm estate** and walk forward to another stile. After dropping more steeply beside the **Sugarloaf**, the way continues along a narrow meadow to **Dale Farm**.

For a short detour, take the ongoing track down to the river at **Wetton Mill**.

5. Return along the track to **Dale Farm**, and turn left along a gated track signed to 'Hulme End'.

Eventually a riverside dovecote and **Swainsley House** come into view on the opposite bank, while beside the path is the gated entrance to a sough, a tunnel dug deep into the hillside to drain the copper mines.

6. Meeting a lane, turn left and walk across **Ecton Bridge**, taking the right fork just beyond. As the lane then swings abruptly to the portal of a tunnel, dug to take the Leek and Manifold Light Railway through the hillside, turn right onto the **Manifold Trail**.

Beyond a small car park, look for the exposed rock faces beside the track. *They show the intricate layering and folding of the strata, some of which are rich in fossils.*

After later crossing the river, the trail winds past the Ecton ore dressing floors to meet the lane at **Dale Bridge**. Cross the lane and carry on along the trail back to **Hulme End**, to finish. ♦

Limestone fossils

The Manifold limestone was formed some 330 million years ago by the deposition of countless shells, corals and sediment in tropical seas. Fossil-rich rocks beside the path contain brachiopods, creatures with upper and lower shells, and a projecting pedicle, or foot, by which they attached to a rock. The name comes from the Greek, meaning arm foot, but they are sometimes known as 'lamp shells' from their shape.

Sunlight and shade in Wolfscote Dale

Hartington & Wolfscote Dale

A beautiful walk through two very different dales in the heart of the White Peak

What to expect:
Easy walking on good tracks and field paths

Distance: 9km/5¾ miles. Allow 3 hours

Start: Mill Lane pay and display car park, Hartington

Grid ref: SK 127 602

Ordnance Survey Map: Explorer OL24 *Peak District: White Peak area: Buxton, Bakewell, Matlock & Dovedale*

After the walk: Pubs and tearooms in Hartington; or the Village Store sells pastries and sandwiches

Walk outline

The walk leaves Hartington past the Youth Hostel, climbing over the flank of Wolfscote Hill and into Biggin Dale. It wanders through the valley to its junction with Wolfscote Dale and then follows the River Dove upstream past Frank i'th Rocks Bridge into Beresford Dale. Leaving the river beyond Pike Pool, the route takes to the fields, passing below the low hillock of Pennilow on its way back to the village.

Hartington's dales

The River Dove is often claimed to be the Peak's prettiest river, its valley changing character as it cuts a winding course through the limestone plateau. Along the stretch encountered here, the narrow, craggy dale of Wolfscote contrasts with the broad meadows and woodland of upper Beresford Dale. Before reaching the Dove, however, the route wanders through lesser known Biggin Dale. It's generally dry, but following prolonged rain, a stream may run in the lower section. Spring is particularly beautiful, when wildflowers add delicate colours to the grass and scree slopes. Marjoram, cowslip and scabious abound, but look out for others such as the rare Jacob's ladder.

Wolfscote Dale

Jacob's ladder

The Walk

1. Walk left from the car park into **Hartington village**, keeping right with the main lane towards Ashbourne. At the junction just past the village store, turn right again to climb away.

Hartington is a pretty medieval market village on the River Dove once associated with mining and Stilton cheese. Notable buildings around the village green include a fine Perpendicular church, the old town hall, school house and cheese shop.

2. Passing the **youth hostel**, leave along a walled track on the right signed to 'Hulme End and Dove Dale'. At a junction, keep ahead through a gate, the track shortly ending into a field. Bear right, crossing a broken wall at the far side and continuing into the corner, where a stile gives onto **Raynards Lane**.

3. Go left to a sharp bend and take the track ahead, keeping with the right branch as it immediately forks, the way signed to 'Biggin Dale'.

After passing a large abandoned barn, the track begins a gentle descent towards the fold of a valley. Through a final gate, the way drops more steeply to the base of the dale.

4. Turn right towards the confluence with **Biggin Dale**. There, look for a gate on the left. Pass through and swing right around a **walled dew pond**. *The underlying limestone is porous and so in the past farmers created these lined circular ponds to water their livestock.*

Wolfscote Dale: *The scree-edged path beside the River Dove in Wolfscote Dale*

Continue along Biggin Dale, the way now signed to 'Wolfscote Dale'. Biggin Dale is a wildflower-rich national nature reserve cared for by the National Trust. Grass and bare scree on the steep flanks soon give way to woodland where ash and hawthorn predominate.

Leaving the trees behind, watch for a small stile in front of a cave. *It is in fact the entrance to an adit, dug as a trial in search of lead ore.*

Shortly, the sound of water heralds your approach to **Wolfscote Dale**.

5. Turn right to follow the valley upstream, passing beneath soaring pinnacles of rock and tongues of scree, known here as *slitherbanks*. The **River Dove** is stepped in a succession of weirs, creating pools for the trout.

6. Reaching **Frank i'th Rocks Bridge**, remain on this bank and continue through a squeeze stile across a riverside meadow. At the far side is another bridge. Cross and turn right into the wooded gorge of **Beresford Dale**.

Misty morn: *A low autumn mist hangs over the fields south of Hartington*

Approaching a third bridge, the deep pool is known as **Pike Pool**. It's named not for the fish but the moss-covered spike of rock that rises above it.

Wolfscote Dale is intimately linked to the 17th-century poet and writer Charles Cotton. He was born at Beresford Hall, which overlooked the gorge from the western bank above Pike Pool. During the 19th century, the hall fell into ruin and a tower, which can be glimpsed from the path below, was built over its foundations in 1905.

Cotton penned an 86-page poem describing 'The Wonders of the Peake'. Published in 1861, his wonders comprised: "Poole Cavern, St Anne's Well at Buxton, Tydes Well, Eldon Hole, Mam Tor, Peake's Arse [an old name for Peak Cavern at Castleton] and the 'stately and stupendous pile' of Chatworth [Chatsworth]". It was one of the first guide books to popularise the area and, directing travellers to the must-see sights, became the basis for a Grand Tour.

After re-crossing the water, the path soon leaves the river, rising through **Morson Wood** to emerge onto pasture.

7. A clear trod strikes away, curving past the base of **Pennilow** to a gate. Carry on through a second wall, rising towards a gated stile. Cross a walled track and continue at the edge of a final field behind a farm.

Emerging at the edge of **Hartington village**, turn right and then go left back to the car park to complete the walk. ♦

Izaak Walton

Charles Cotton of nearby Beresford Hall was a close friend of Izaak Walton, the father of modern fishing. He introduced him to the delights of fishing the Dove for trout. They also spent many an hour in Cotton's fishing temple in Beresford Dale. Izaak Walton's classic book, The Compleat Angler was written in the 1600s but is still in print today. Its closing lines advise that all true fishermen should 'Study to be quiet'.

The famous stepping stones at Dove Dale

Dove Dale

A walk through the Peak's most famous dale from a picturesque Victorian estate village

Distance/time: 10.5km/6½ miles. Allow 3½ hours

Start: Ilam Hall, National Trust pay and display car park

Grid ref: SK 131 507

Ordnance Survey Map: Explorer OL24 *Peak District: White Peak area: Buxton, Bakewell, Matlock & Dovedale*

After the walk: National Trust visitor centre and tearoom at Ilam Hall

Walk outline

The path from Ilam skirts the western flank of Bunster Hill, passing a crystal stream emanating from St Bertram's Well. After briefly following a quiet lane, the way crosses fields to the head of Hall Dale, a secluded, dry valley that leads to Dove Dale. A riverside path winds through the gorge below towering rock formations. The final leg crosses grazing pastures behind the Izaak Walton Hotel back to the village.

Dove Dale

Tourists have been flocking to Dove Dale since the 18th century, awed by the soaring rock pillars and sheer cliffs lining the narrow gorge. The different features became endowed with Romantic names, some even acquiring an embellishing tale or two. At Lover's Leap, a maiden threw herself into the gorge in despair on hearing of her lover's death but, caught in a tree, she lived, to learn that he too was happily alive. Reynard was a local brigand and the cave his hideout, but tragedy struck when an inquisitive Victorian visitor was killed in attempting to ride his horse up the steep path.

Reynard's Cave

White-letter hairstreak

The Walk

1. Walk back along the main drive of Ilam Hall and continue ahead through the village to the **memorial cross**.

Fork left, but leave left after 200 metres through a small gate onto **Bunster Hill**.

2. Climb forward past the National Trust plaque to a signboard and carry on, picking up a field track towards Stanshope. Over a stile beside a gate, continue up the rising base of a shallow valley.

The intermittent stream is from **St Bertram's Well**; named for an 8th-century Mercian prince who renounced his wealth and position to live as a hermit. In the next pasture, make for a stile near the top right corner. Bear left above the wall, following it to a squeeze stile.

3. Walk forward to another crossing near the wall corner. Strike a diagonal route across the next large field, later passing above the hollow of an **old quarry** to a stile in the end wall. Keep the same line, crossing a track and then leaving over the lefthand wall onto **Ilam-moor Lane**.

4. Head up the hill. As the lane begins to fall, look for a stile immediately beyond a gate on the right.

5. Diagonal paths criss-cross the field; look for a stile out

Colossal curve: *A vast, water-eroded limestone arch guards Reynard's Cave*

at the top right corner near a derelict barn. Follow a track through gates passing the barn and then a **dewpond**. Beyond a gate at the very end, go left to a second gate.

Walking away, look back to see a lime kiln built into the hillside below a small quarry. The footpath stays beside the lefthand wall, but there are dramatic views into Hall Dale if you follow the fenceline over to the right instead. Fence and wall eventually meet at a stile.

Continue down a steep, grassy bank, which may be slippery in wet weather.

6. Over a stile at the bottom, turn right into **Hall Dale**. The path descends gently through the valley; the steep sides are initially bare, but farther on, become wooded on the right. Larch gives way to ash as the dale narrows, the accompanying wall thickly enveloped in moss. Rounding a corner, the **River Dove** can be heard and the path drops into the main valley. Turn downstream, shortly crossing a bridge below the lofty pinnacle of **Ilam Rock**.

Popular dale: *Looking up Dove Dale from just above the famous stepping stones*

If you have time, there is a pretty 1.5 kilometre, or 1 mile, diversion upstream to Milldale (**7**) and **Viator's Bridge,** which is mentioned in Izaak Walton's classic 17th-century fishing treatise, *The Compleat Angler*. Return to this point to resume the walk downstream.

8. Continuing beside the river, the path resorts to a causeway as the gorge dramatically narrows. Where the dale later widens, look up left to see a splendid **natural arch**, behind which is **Reynard's Cave**. The path then climbs onto the rocky viewpoint of **Lover's Leap**, the stone steps full of fossilised crinoids, ancient sea creatures similar to the present-day sea lily. The path soon returns to the river, passing weirs containing shallow pools for trout.

9. As the main gorge swings right in front of **Lin Dale**, Victorian **stepping stones** cross the river. Alternatively, there is a bridge a little farther downstream.

10. Reaching the entrance to the **Dove Dale car park**, bear right through a gate into the overflow car park, leaving right again in a few metres through trees to a stile.

trike out behind the **Izaak Walton Hotel**, pausing to look back at the runcated pyramid of Thorpe Cloud. Over a couple of stiles, keep going cross another large field. Beyond its far-left corner, **Ilam Hall** appears ahead, a developing track leading into a final pasture. Towards the end, drop left to the lane and go back through the village to complete the walk. ♦

Ilam memorial cross

The village cross at Ilam is a memorial erected by Jesse Watts-Russell to his wife Mary. Given the Ilam estate as a wedding present by his father, Jesse built the Gothic hall and laid out the model estate village. The memorial takes the form of an Eleanor Cross, of which twelve were commissioned by Edward I to mark resting-places on the route from Lincoln along which his wife's body was taken for interment at Westminster Abbey.

Useful Information

Visit Peak District & Derbyshire

The Peak's official tourism website covers everything from accommodation and special events to attractions and adventure. **www.visitpeakdistrict.com**

Peak District National Park

The Peak District National Park website also has information on things to see and do plus a host of practical details to help plan your visit. **www.peakdistrict.org**

Tourist Information Centres

The main TICs provide free information on everything from accommodation and transport to what's on and walking advice..

Bakewell	01629 816558	bakewell@peakdistrict.gov.uk
Castleton	01629 816572	castleton@peakdistrict.gov.uk
Moorland Centre, Edale	01433 670207	edale@peakdistrict.gov.uk
Upper Derwent	01433 650953	derwentinfo@peakdistrict.gov.uk

Weather

Online weather forecasts for the Peak District are available from the Met Office at **www.metoffice.gov.uk/loutdoor/mountainsafety/** and the Mountain Weather Information Service at **www.mwis.org.uk/**

Rail Travel

Four railway service cross the National Park:

The Hope Valley Line

The Derwent Valley Line

The Manchester to Buxton Line

The Manchester to Glossop Line

Information is available from National Rail Enquiries on 08457 484950 or **www. nationalrail.com.uk**

Bus Travel

Peakland's towns and many of the villages are served by bus. Information is available from Traveline on 0871 200 22 33 or **www.traveline.info**